Forgiveness & Hope
40 Daily Devotionals for the Incarcerated from the Book of Psalms

David W. Smith

DEDICATION

This book is dedicated to all the men and women who are incarceration, their loved ones and those that support them, especially my family who stood by me with forgiveness and compassion.

CONTENTS

INTRODUCTION

When the cell door shut behind me I was alone. I didn't even have a Bible. Eventually the chaplain's aide visited me with a Bible. I knew I needed to hear God's words of forgiveness and hope so I turned to Psalms, the book that, as a pastor, I'd always pointed people to during their time of need. When I turned to those words of hope I found despair instead. The only hope was for the righteous and I was far from righteousness, or so I thought.

It took some time but God slowly reminded me that His love for me isn't based on how I lived my life, my righteousness, but His compassion. My forgiveness isn't based on the life I lived but on the life, death and resurrection that Jesus lived.

These devotions are meditations on the Psalms. 40 days of hope and forgiveness. I hope and pray that through them God will reveal His forgiveness for you and the hope it brings. You will discover freedom through faith and knowledge that your relationship with God isn't based on what you've done in your past but what God does for you, everyday.

David Smith

DAY 1

PRAISE GOD!

PSALM 30:1-5

Do you feel like you can praise God right now? I'm sitting in a jail cell and, let's be honest, it's hard to praise God. My freedom is gone, my life has been wrecked and I'm still supposed to praise God?

Does what you're experiencing today make praising God hard? Now is the time to look to His promises for you!

This passage from Psalms is filled with promises of God's action in the life of a sinner. God has "drawn me up" (v1), "healed me" (v2) and "restored me to life." (v3)

This is a hard change. Instead of focusing on our present struggles God calls us to see His eternal reality. It's not natural, but that's why God gives us His Holy Spirit. The Holy Spirit strengthens and comforts us when we struggle. The Holy Spirit lets us know that the suffering is only temporary but God's Love for us is eternal!

Look at your life right now. No matter how bad you feel like things are you are still alive. God's anger may be on you for a moment because of your sin BUT His blessings are forever! (v5) Let's praise God for that!

PRAYER

Oh Wonderful God!

You are worthy of all my praise and honor. Send Your Holy Spirit to me so when I suffer I will see it is temporary and know Your love for me is eternal so that I will always praise Your name!

In Jesus Name I pray,

Amen

I will extol you, O LORD, for you have drawn me up and have not let my foes rejoice over me. O LORD my God, I cried to you for help, and you have healed me. O LORD, you have brought up my soul from Sheol; you restored me to life from among those who go down to the pit. Sing praises to the LORD, O you his saints, and give thanks to his holy name. For his anger is but for a moment, and his favor is for a lifetime. Weeping may tarry for the night, but joy comes with the morning.

Psalms 30:1-5

REFLECTIONS

DAY 2

CHANGING PRAISE

PSALM 30:11-12

Would you say your life is one where you're mourning or dancing? As I write this I'm sitting in my jail cell in December looking at Christmas pictures of my three children whom I haven't seen for almost a year (and won't see in person for another three years). Mourning would be an understatement of my current feelings! Can you identify with my feeling of loss because of sin? Are you mourning something in your life now?

Mourning is a strong emotion. There's a deep sadness, some might even say depression. But our mourning won't last forever!

As unbelievable as it may seem today, God will change your mourning into a celebration! This happens when our eyes are opened to the greatness of God's work. My separation that causes my mourning is only temporary. Not only that, God has used this sad season in my life to strengthen my faith.

Your situation is only temporary, too. God sent Jesus, His own Son, to die for you. God's not going to abandon you now! God can use this sad season in your life to change you so you can praise Him forever!

PRAYER

Gracious God,

I am full of sorrow because of my sin and suffering. Help me to see Your continual love for me so that my mourning might be transformed into rejoicing in Christ!

In Jesus name,

Amen

You have turned for me my mourning into dancing; you have loosed my sackcloth and clothed me with gladness, that my glory may sing your praise and not be silent. O LORD my God, I will give thanks to you forever!
Psalms 30:11-12

REFLECTIONS

DAY 3

THE TRUTH OF MY SITUATION

PSALM 103:6-10

Do you feel the bad things in your life are permanent? Does your punishment feel like it will never end? We have a hard time seeing beyond where we are right now. When times are good we can't imagine things being bad and when times get bad it's easy to quickly give up hope. But what's the truth of my situation?

God does strive against us sometimes but it won't last forever. (v9) He is angry because of our sins, but He won't be that way forever. His anger has a purpose: to turn us away from our sin and to make us remember how bad our sins are so we won't do it again. We will think His anger is too much but when we compare it to what should happen to us because of our sin – DEATH – we realize God is merciful!

In His mercy God sent His son to pay the cost to redeem us from our sins. In His mercy God sends His Holy Spirit to guide and comfort us. In His mercy God reminds us our suffering is temporary but our joy in the Lord is eternal!

PRAYER

Dear Loving Father,

At times I feel like the trials in my life are permanent and I have no chance for peace or joy. But You know the truth! You know that no matter how bad my current situation is it is only temporary and You can use it to build my faith in You! Let my faith be built in You!

Thank you!

In Jesus Name I pray,

Amen

The LORD works righteousness and justice for all who are oppressed. He made known his ways to Moses, his acts to the people of Israel. The LORD is merciful and gracious, slow to anger and abounding in steadfast love. He will not always chide, nor will he keep his anger forever. He does not deal with us according to our sins, nor repay us according to our iniquities.

Psalms 103:6-10

REFLECTIONS

DAY 4

FAR AWAY

PSALM 103:11-14

The only window in my cell is in a door. On the top of the wall opposite my cell are narrow windows. Because of how high I am in downtown jail when I look out the window all I can see are the tops of sky scrapers and the occasional plane that flies by in the distance.

I'm so far away from the planes I can't even make out its windows. The people on that plane are so far away that they probably can't tell this high rise is a jail and even if they could they wouldn't be able to tell that I'm looking at them. We are so far away from each other that neither of us can have any power or influence over the other.

Take that same distance and multiply it by infinity and that's how far God has removed your sins from you. He's moved them so far away that your sins won't determine if you will be loved by God. Jesus' blood on the cross, the faith God gives you and the new life you have through baptism determine God's love for you! And that is far and away better than relying on your sinful past!

PRAYER

Oh Gracious God,

No matter how heavy my sins feel to me you move them away from me as far as the East is from the west. You have moved them so far away that they can no longer hurt me! Thank You for Your loving care!

In Jesus Name I pray,

Amen

For as high as the heavens are above the earth, so great is his steadfast love toward those who fear him; as far as the east is from the west, so far does he remove our transgressions from us. As a father shows compassion to his children, so the LORD shows compassion to those who fear him. For he knows our frame; he remembers that we are dust.

Psalms 103:11-14

REFLECTIONS

David Smith

DAY 5

THE BLESSING OF SURVIVAL

PSALM 66:10-15

Do you ever look at your life and wonder how you've managed to survive? You think about what you've done and what's happened to you and you think, "How am I still standing?"

We've all done some bad things and suffered some bad consequences. But God didn't give you those consequences to break you. He gave them to you to refine you as "silver is tried." (v10)

How is a metal tried, or refined? By superheating it so the impurities separate from the metal. Do you think superheating is a painless or easy process? Of course it isn't! And neither is getting rid of your sin.

The consequences you suffer because of your sin are painful. The consequences Jesus suffered through, to the point of death, were painful. The consequences are painful but they don't threaten your survival.

God wants you to not just survive but thrive after you've been refined!

Since you've been refined (turned from your sin and left it behind) through the power of God's Holy Spirit giving you faith in Christ and cleaning you in Baptism, you can offer God the gift of your praise and service! God has changed you for good so now you can give him the goodness He has given you!

PRAYER

Oh, Almighty God,

Thank you for helping me survive Your refining fires. You make me holy through Jesus' death and the power of the Holy Spirit. In my new life help me share the blessings You have given me,

In the merciful name of Jesus I pray,

Amen

For you, O God, have tested us; you have tried us as silver is tried. You brought us into the net; you laid a crushing burden on our backs; you let men ride over our heads; we went through fire and through water; yet you have brought us out to a place of abundance. I will come into your house with burnt offerings; I will perform my vows to you, that which my lips uttered and my mouth promised when I was in trouble. I will offer to you burnt offerings of fattened animals, with the smoke of the sacrifice of rams; I will make an offering of bulls and goats.

Psalms 66:10-15

REFLECTIONS

DAY 6

REJOICING IN THE LAW

PSALM 19:7-11

Rejoicing in the law probably isn't the first thing that comes to your mind since you were arrested. It's probably the furthest thing from it. Since God gives authority to rulers of nations when we break the law of the land we break God's law.

But that's why we should rejoice in the law-not because it punishes but because it guides us to God. It converts us from lost sinners to saints found by God!

When we leave sin by being born again by God the law that once condemned us now guides us. It shows us how to love God! It keeps us clean by showing us how to avoid the deadly filth of Satan's sinful tricks. God's law is what we end up desiring!

When we strive for the Law we have peace in our lives. Why? We don't get in trouble for breaking the law since we're following it. Also, we have the joy of living a life filled with the Holy Spirit that pleases God.

With the Holy Spirit and peace because of the law we can rejoice!

PRAYER

Oh Loving God,

Before you redeemed me the law could only condemn me. But now that I'm Your born-again child Your law is my guide. Help me rejoice in the peace and freedom that comes from following Your law.

In Jesus Name I Pray,

Amen

The law of the LORD is perfect, reviving the soul; the testimony of the LORD is sure, making wise the simple; the precepts of the LORD are right, rejoicing the heart; the commandment of the LORD is pure, enlightening the eyes; the fear of the LORD is clean, enduring forever; the rules of the LORD are true, and righteous altogether. More to be desired are they than gold, even much fine gold; sweeter also than honey and drippings of the honeycomb. Moreover, by them is your servant warned; in keeping them there is great reward.

Psalms 19:7-11

REFLECTIONS

DAY 7

SECRET FAULTS

PSLAM 19:12

As I've been recovering from addiction and living a sober life my memory has surprised me-and not in a good way! I rack my brain, retrace my steps, and try to piece together the past so I can be honest with myself, the people I've hurt and God. However, it seems like every time I remember everything a new clue appears that reminds me of another past sin. Eventually, I pray, I'll discover all those secret faults so I can make amends and move forward.

But there's another type of secret faults, the ones we don't even understand! A common prayer for God's forgiveness includes the confession of sins "known and unknown." That prayer recognizes we do things that are sins against God and we don't even realize it! Usually it's because it's so much a part of the culture we live in that we can't see it. But even if we don't recognize it as a sin, it still separates us from God.

That's why David prays to be cleansed from secret faults. We need the blood of Christ to wash away all our sins-including the ones we're hiding from or don't recognize. Then God won't remember them anymore!

PRAYER

All Knowing God,

You know all my sins-the ones I confess, the ones I'm hiding from and the ones I don't even recognize. Father, I beg Your forgiveness for all these sins. Cleanse me from all my faults so I can joyfully praise Your name!

In Jesus Name I Pray,

Amen

Who can discern his errors? Declare me innocent from hidden faults.
Psalms 19:12

REFLECTIONS

DAY 8

SEEKING GOD

PSLAM 34:4-7

"Seeking God" is an odd idea. If God is all knowing, all powerful, and everywhere why would we need to seek Him? How could he wander off from us?

We must seek God not because He wandered off from us but because we wandered off from Him. Every time we sinned we took a step away from Him. Every time we did things our way instead of God's way we took a step away from Him. With each step we took out of God's presence we separated ourselves more from God's Love. The further we were separated from God's love the easier it became to step away from God because we were beginning to forget what it was like to feel God's love.

Then, one day, we realize something's not right. We look for God and He's not there. Since we separated ourselves from God now we must seek God!

But as soon as we seek God He'll find us! He doesn't make us wander back to Him but He sends His angels to us to bring us back. He delivers us from our fears, our sins and Satan because even in your sin God is seeking you!

PRAYER

Oh All-Knowing God,

In my sin I have wandered off from You and have lost You. Hear my cry as I call out to You. Send Your angels to protect me and bring me back to You!

In Jesus Name I Pray,

Amen

I sought the LORD, and he answered me and delivered me from all my fears. Those who look to him are radiant, and their faces shall never be ashamed. This poor man cried, and the LORD heard him and saved him out of all his troubles. The angel of the LORD encamps around those who fear him, and delivers them.

Psalms 34:4-7

REFLECTIONS

DAY 9

I AM RIGHTEOUS

PSALM 34:17

Do you feel righteous? Probably not.

Sometimes we might feel self-righteous, proud. Rarely do we feel righteous, like we have honored God with our lives as He has called us to do. Look at your life. How often have you been righteous on your own? If we are brutally honest it doesn't matter how good we think we are or how good someone acts, none of us are righteous on our own. If none are righteous on our own who can share in this promise from God: "The righteous cry out and the Lord hears and delivers them out of all their troubles."(v17) It seems like we, since we're all unrighteous, would have no hope of deliverance. That would be true, if it weren't for God's love.

When you were baptized you were united with Christ in His death and resurrection. That means you now share in His life-including His righteousness! The righteousness of God is also our righteousness!

Now when you cry out to God He hears you because He no longer sees Your sins, He only sees Christ's righteousness covering you. You can have confidence that God will be with you to save you and sustain you because He always keeps His promises.

PRAYER

Oh Righteous God,

In my sin I can feel unworthy of Your love. Send Your Holy Spirit to remind me that because You have washed me in the waters of Christ's baptism I now share in Christ's righteousness and all the promises that includes!

In Jesus Name I Pray,

Amen

When the righteous cry for help, the LORD hears and delivers them out of all their troubles.
Psalms 34:17

REFLECTIONS

DAY 10

LISTENING GOD

PSALM 66:16-20

What does it take for someone to listen to you? Do you have to prove your smarts? Maybe people only listen if you make it worth their time. Do you think the only way someone will listen to you is if you intimidate them?

When you try to get people to listen using these tricks it doesn't work to well, does it? People start to resent you and then you get mad and pretty soon nobody is listening to anyone anymore. When you treat God the same way you treat others He won't listen to you either.

When you try to boast, deal or argue with God to make Him hear you He won't listen. You've turned your back to Him when you act that way. Instead of walking with God you're walking away from God. The further away you get, the angrier and more scared you get, and the more demanding you get with God. It's a deadly cycle!

But if you stop "cherish[ing] iniquity in [your] heart" (v18) by turning from your sin God will hear you and bring you back to Him!

God hears your prayer. God brings you back to His mercy. God listens to and loves you!

PRAYER

Oh, Merciful God,

When I speak prideful or harshly to You I turn myself away from Your love. Send Your Holy Spirit to soften my words so that You will hear my prayer and bring me out of my sin and into Your love.

In Jesus Name I Pray,

Amen

Come and hear, all you who fear God, and I will tell what he has done for my soul. I cried to him with my mouth, and high praise was on my tongue. If I had cherished iniquity in my heart, the Lord would not have listened. But truly God has listened; he has attended to the voice of my prayer. Blessed be God, because he has not rejected my prayer or removed his steadfast love from me!

Psalms 66:16-20

REFLECTIONS

DAY 11

PLUGGING UP SIN'S HOLES

PSALM 19:12-13

Have you ever noticed how sin has a way of creeping into our lives? It's like we build up an earthen levy to protect us from the flood waters of sin. We look out at the destructive forces of sin on the other side and pride ourselves that we're protected.

But, we miss the water seeping through our levy. Those presumptuous sins creep in and make holes in our protective levy. Slowly our defenses against sin are weakened until the levee fails and the flood waters of sin come rushing in to destroy! Oh, if only I had seen my sin!

But God knows our secret faults, our weaknesses. He sees the sins we ignore or deny. Even after we feel hopeless and washed away He is there to forgive us! His Holy Spirit plugs up the holes, stopping Satan's destruction. There is one water more powerful than the flood waters of sin. It is the Holy Spirit with the drowning waters of baptism. Our sins are drowned and washed away. Forgiveness comes to us because of Christ on the cross when God unites us to Him in faith and baptism. Our weak spots are plugged up, reinforced, as we rest in God's power instead of our own presumptuousness.

PRAYER

Dear Lord,

When I confess my sins to You open my eyes to all my sins, even those I'm hiding from. Give me awareness to turn away from them and freedom to follow You instead.

In Jesus Name I Pray,

Amen

Who can discern his errors? Declare me innocent from hidden faults. Keep back your servant also from presumptuous sins; let them not have dominion over me! Then I shall be blameless, and innocent of great transgression.

Psalms 19:12-13

REFLECTIONS

David Smith

DAY 12

WHAT HAVE I SAID?

PSALM 19:14

How have your words hurt yourself or others? Have they landed you in jail? Have they broken relationships with people you love? Have your words separated you from God? The old saying, "Sticks and stones may break my bones but words will never hurt me," is probably the biggest lie we tell ourselves. Words are powerful! When they come out of my mouth they can be a powerful force that destroys everything in their path, including myself.

That's why today's verse is so important. "Let the words of my mouth and the meditation of my heart be acceptable in your sight." David desires for His words to please God!

Why are God pleasing words so important? When we honor and please God with our words we are praising Him and bringing peace in to our lives. We praise God not just with "Alleluias" or "amens" but every time we allow the Holy Spirit to conform our words to God's will. When our words are acceptable to God we receive peace because we are in union with Him.

Think of all the strife your words have caused in your life. Now, imagine how much more peace you would have if you had said God pleasing words. Those are powerful words!

PRAYER

Gracious Lord,

I often let Satan control my words so they hurt others and myself while separating me from You. This isn't what I want! Send Your Holy Spirit to strengthen me and let the words of my mouth and the meditation of my heart be acceptable in Your sight, O Lord, my rock and my redeemer.

In Jesus Name I Pray,

Amen

Let the words of my mouth and the meditation of my heart be acceptable in your sight, O LORD, my rock and my redeemer.
Psalms 19:14

REFLECTIONS

DAY 13

MAKING ENEMIES

PSALM 139:19-22

There is a popular of image of God as a good buddy who loves everyone no matter what. People think of God as an overly generous friend who is blind to all their sins. Nothing could be further from the truth.

God will forgive your sins because of the blood of Jesus when you repent but not everyone wants to repent. How many of your friends are living in unrepentant sin. The devil uses your time around people like that to pull you away from God's love and promises! How many of your current problems stem from whom you spend time around?

To change our lives we must change the people, places and things that took us away from God. Getting rid of bad "friends" is changing people. In today's Psalm David wants to get the "blood thirsty" (v19) men out of his life. He "loathes" and has a "perfect hatred" (v22) for God's enemies. David realizes he needs to be totally separated from evil in order to grow in God's love.

As time goes on and God strengthens your faith and heals your wounds from Satan's attacks then you can return to these "friends" as one might warrior with the redeeming Gospel

PRAYER

Dear Lord,

You are my best friend. You are there when I need comfort and strength. You rejoice with me and you weep with me. Separate me, I pray, from "friends" who would pull me away from Your love. Strengthen me in their absence so one day You might send me to them with Your Gospel.

In Jesus Name I Pray,

Amen

Oh that you would slay the wicked, O God! O men of blood, depart from me! They speak against you with malicious intent; your enemies take your name in vain. Do I not hate those who hate you, O LORD? And do I not loathe those who rise up against you? I hate them with complete hatred; I count them my enemies.

Psalms 139:19-22

REFLECTIONS

DAY 14

PARDONED

PSALM 25:11

Have you ever received a pardon for you crimes? Few do, but most every day I hope and pray my lawyer has worked some judicial miracle so I could be released from jail and probation. I doubt this will ever happen. I pled guilty and received a just and fair sentence according to the guidelines and now I have to suffer the consequences. You've probably ended up in a similar circumstance-your sin has brought some painful consequences. Not just through the judicial system but also I in your daily life through broken trust and broken relationships. Even in the consequences present in our daily life it can be hard for people to forgive, or pardon, you. With the lack of forgiveness Satan can deceive us into thinking God won't pardon us, either.

But the Psalmist shows us we can call on God to pardon us. In Christ's crucifixion God kept His promise to forgive us. We're not waiting and hoping for a call that will never come. As baptized believers in Christ, once we confess our sins God faithfully and immediately forgives us. Just like the Psalmist we can have confidence in God's pardoning forgiveness.

PRAYER

Gracious God,

Pardons are rare in our society so it is hard for me to believe that you willing took the punishment for my sin and pardoned me the minute I confessed. Send me Your Holy Spirit to strengthen me so I may continually believe in Your pardoning love.

In Jesus Name I Pray,

Amen

For your name's sake, O LORD, pardon my guilt, for it is great.
Psalms 25:11

REFLECTIONS

DAY 15

BEING FOUND

PSALM 119:175-176

As soon as the police know you've broken the law the police are looking for you. We don't want to get caught. We want to hide. We don't want to admit our guilt (or be found guilty!). We don't want to suffer the consequences of breaking the law, of sinning. We would rather live in fear than take steps to move forward.

Our relationship with God is the same. When we sin how often do we go to God and say, "Hey, I'm sorry about what I did. Can You help me not do this again?"

No, our normal reaction is the opposite. We won't confess our sins. We're filled with guilt, shame or fear. We do our best to hide from God!

Does God forget about us? No!

Just like the police searching for a criminal, God searches for us until He finds us! When God finds you He takes you from Satan's place of deadly fear and revives you with new life by the forgiveness found in Christ's blood. God helps us remember His commandments which bring life. God, as was His plan from the beginning, brings us to a place of life and joy where we praise God both here and through eternity!

PRAYER

Loving Father,

Thank You for seeking me when Satan led me astray! Now that You have found me, remove my sin and teach me Your commandments so I may live a life praising You!

In Jesus Name I Pray,

Amen

Let my soul live and praise you, and let your rules help me. I have gone astray like a lost sheep; seek your servant, for I do not forget your commandments.

Psalms 119:175-176

REFLECTIONS

DAY 16

HOPE WHEN YOU'RE DOWN

PSALM 42:5-6

"Take one day at a time." These words of wisdom were preached to me over and over during the seven months between my arrest and sentencing. While well intentioned, they missed the reality of what was happening in my life and anyone's life who is experiencing the horrible consequences of sin. By saying, "take one day at a time" people were encouraging me to stay in the present. But where is my hope in the present?

My present is filled with sin and its consequences. I'm living the reality of being separated from God because I let a sneaky Satan deceive me. Like the psalmist, my soul was cast down and I was in turmoil. When you're down you have no hope in the present, only in the future because of the past.

Our hope when we're crushed by sin is grounded in the past reality of Jesus' death for our sin. Our hope is fulfilled in the future restoration when we will live in the presence of God because of His saving grace! In the middle of our present suffering hope can be hard to feel but God has proclaimed His present promise of Hope, first for the Israelites and now for you!

PRAYER

All Mighty God,

When the present reality of the consequences of my sin has me in so much turmoil that I am cast down lift me up in the hope of the cross that restores me through Your forgiving love.

In Jesus Name I Pray,

Amen

Why are you cast down, O my soul, and why are you in turmoil within me? Hope in God; for I shall again praise him, my salvation and my God. My soul is cast down within me; therefore I remember you from the land of Jordan and of Hermon, from Mount Mizar.

Psalms 42:5-6

REFLECTIONS

DAY 17

KEEPING SCORE

PSALM 130:1-4

I'm a competitive guy so I like to keep score. I want to know if I'm winning or figure out who is so I can learn from that person. Sometimes, when I realize I don't have the skill to win I'll make sure we don't keep score and stop trying. That way I can hide my shortcomings.

When it came to my "sin scorecard" I did the same thing. I realized I couldn't win-there was no way I could stop sinning and "beat" Jesus' perfect record so I stopped keeping score and stopped trying. That's just what Satan wanted!

When I stopped trying to follow the example of Jesus and other saints the only option was to follow Satan and his lies. Maybe you've done the same thing. All too soon you are trapped by Satan's lies and in the depths of sin. You see yourself and think you've lost the game of life.

But when we cry "Mercy!" from the depths of sin and loss *God hears us!* God knows on our own we could never stand as winners. But with God there is forgiveness and new life! That's because the only score that matters is: God Won-Satan Zero.

PRAYER

Lord God,

I cannot match Your perfection in order to stand before You. However, through Christ's death and resurrection You have forgiven my sins so I can now share perfection with You. Thank you for winning for m!

In Jesus Name I Pray,

Amen

Out of the depths I cry to you, O LORD! O Lord, hear my voice! Let your ears be attentive to the voice of my pleas for mercy! If you, O LORD, should mark iniquities, O Lord, who could stand? But with you there is forgiveness, that you may be feared.
Psalms 130:1-4

REFLECTIONS

DAY 18

GOD'S BASIS FOR JUDGEMENT

PSALM 143:1-6

Imagine going before a judge for sentencing. You've already been found guilty and now it's up to you to convince that judge not to lock you up and throw away the key. What can you do? You can't say you didn't do it-you've already been found guilty. You can't claim "good character" not after what you did. You can't claim you'll never do it again-no one would believe you. Really, you have no control. It's either the wrath or mercy of the judge.

We're in the same situation with God. Our sins convict us. Satan has crushed us in sin so we have nothing of our own to claim. If we remind God of our own deeds we would be sentenced to an eternal separation from God because we aren't good enough. But we can remind God of what Jesus did for us. His death separated us from our sin when God pronounces our sentence. Now, when we pray to God, God hears our please for mercy! God remembers Christ's blood shed on the cross for us. He mercifully frees us from our sentence of eternal incarceration. Not because of our works but because of His!

PRAYER

Oh Merciful God,

If you were to sentence me based on my life and what I'm capable of doing You would justly sentence me to an eternal separation from You. But You have shown me mercy in Christ. Every day remind me of Your love so I may rejoice in the new life You have given me.

In Jesus Name I Pray,

Amen

Hear my prayer, O LORD; give ear to my pleas for mercy! In your faithfulness answer me, in your righteousness! Enter not into judgment with your servant, for no one living is righteous before you. For the enemy has pursued my soul; he has crushed my life to the ground; he has made me sit in darkness like those long dead. Therefore my spirit faints within me; my heart within me is appalled. I remember the days of old; I meditate on all that you have done; I ponder the work of your hands. I stretch out my hands to you; my soul thirsts for you like a parched land. Selah.

Psalms 143:1-6

REFLECTIONS

DAY 19

WAITING ON GOD

PSALM 143:7-8

The most nerve-wracking part of my ordeal with the criminal justice system was the waiting from when I decided to plead guilty to my sentencing. I wanted, maybe even needed, to hear the court's judgment on me so I would know what would happen in my life. I ended up in a mini-depression, petrified because of the unknown. When I finally received my sentence I was relieved. I now knew what my future would hold.

As sinners we can end up fearfully frozen because we're waiting for God's judgment. We know we've sinned. We know we deserve eternal punishment. Now we're just waiting for God to proclaim our sentence.

Except God already did on the cross 2000 years ago.

We don't need to wait on God's answer because in giving Jesus to die for our sins God shows us an eternal unfailing, or steadfast, love. In His love God takes us from our sin and into a community of believers who, guided by the Holy Spirit, follow God's way and together we no longer wait on God to condemn us but joyfully lift our souls to our ever-present savior.

PRAYER

Ever Present Lord,

In my sin I fearfully wait on Your condemning judgment-what I deserve. But in Your steadfast love You answered my sin with the sacrificial love of Jesus! Help me trust in this love and lift my soul to you as I follow Your ways.

In Jesus Name I Pray,

Amen

Answer me quickly, O LORD! My spirit fails! Hide not your face from me, lest I be like those who go down to the pit. Let me hear in the morning of your steadfast love, for in you I trust. Make me know the way I should go, for to you I lift up my soul.

Psalms 143:7-8

REFLECTIONS

DAY 20

NOTHING LEFT BUT GOD

PSALM 73:25-28

"There are no atheists in foxholes."

That old saying shows how when our lives are beyond our control, when there is nothing we can do to protect ourselves or change our situation, we cry out to God because we have nothing left but God.

I've never spent time in a foxhole but I think the feeling of fear and helplessness can be similar to incarceration because of our sin. We have no control. Our enemy, Satan, is out to kill us. We're in a sin and death filled situation beyond our control and we have nothing left but God.

This is the reality Asaph proclaims. All my physical powers fail but I still have God. People who I trusted but led me into sin will die. Yet I still have God.

Take me away from all this sin and destruction and bring me into Your presence, we pray to God. It's good for us to be near God because God is our refuge. When we're near God we're filled with His love so we proclaim to others, "I have nothing left but God-and for that I'm eternally thankful!"

PRAYER

Almighty God,

Whether I'm in a real foxhole or in one I've caused because of sin, let me realize I have nothing but You. You are my stronghold and life giver. Draw me into Your presence so I may always praise you.

In Jesus Name I Pray,

Amen

Whom have I in heaven but you? And there is nothing on earth that I desire besides you. My flesh and my heart may fail, but God is the strength of my heart and my portion forever. For behold, those who are far from you shall perish; you put an end to everyone who is unfaithful to you. But for me it is good to be near God; I have made the Lord GOD my refuge, that I may tell of all your works.

Psalms 73:25-28

REFLECTIONS

DAY 21

OUR IGNORANCE, GOD'S COUNSEL

PSALM 73:21-24

Why did we screw up like we did? Some might call you evil, bad or rotten to the core. These words judge and condemn us as people who have no hope. How can something evil be turned righteous? How can something bad be turned good? How can something rotten be turned pure? These are permanent states of being and since that's what some believe about us that's why they've rejected us.

But how does God see us? God knows more of our worst actions. God knows how embittered we can become. God knows *all* our sins and more than anyone who has condemned us on Earth. It would be reasonable, then, that God would see our failings at an even deeper and unchangeable level

But God doesn't! Instead He sees our ignorance!

God knows that our sinful actions come from us not recognizing the devil's deceit, our despair or our salvation in Christ. Instead of condemning us, God counsels us and brings us out of our ignorance. God takes us by the hand, lifts us out of our sin and brings us into His presence. Despite our evil deeds, bad works and rotten thoughts God restores us to Him because of His love for us.

PRAYER

Oh Righteous Father,

Just as others condemn me, in my ignorance I am deceived into thinking you condemn me, too. Let me experience Your Holy counsel and learn of Your love towards me so I may always rejoice in Your love.

In Jesus Name I Pray,

Amen

When my soul was embittered, when I was pricked in heart, I was brutish and ignorant; I was like a beast toward you. Nevertheless, I am continually with you; you hold my right hand. You guide me with your counsel, and afterward you will receive me to glory.

Psalms 73:21-24

REFLECTIONS

DAY 22

REAL LIFE PRAYER

PSALM 38:1-14

David describes some pretty horrible stuff in his life: wounds that stink and fester (v5), burning sides (v7), being crushed (v8), failing strength (v10), blindness (v10) and abandonment by friends. (v11) Does he blame God or others' evil deeds against him for this?

No. David says it's his fault because of his sin. (v3)

We can identify with David's suffering. Our sins and consequences differ but we share a common pain. Some suffer from gunshot wounds, others from loss of relationships, still more from strained relationships or public shaming. With all the painful consequences of sin it's easy to give up. Life has been painfully hard and God's promises seem so distant-like they're not for me. Like God can't hear me.

But look at David's first words, "O Lord, rebuke me not in Your anger." (v1) This is a real life prayer of David. David's not complaining-he's crying out for mercy! Our prayers to God can be just like this-we can cry out to God in the midst of our suffering and, like David, know that God hears us. We know God hears us because He is our Father and He will always be willing to listen to you.

PRAYER

Oh God Who Always Hears Me,

Let me offer up real life prayers that are honest in how I'm suffering and why I'm suffering. When I confess my sins I know You hear me because of the Holy Spirit and You have the power to heal me! Thank You for hearing me and healing me!

In Jesus Name I Pray,

Amen

A Psalm of David, for the memorial offering. O LORD, rebuke me not in your anger, nor discipline me in your wrath! For your arrows have sunk into me, and your hand has come down on me. There is no soundness in my flesh because of your indignation; there is no health in my bones because of my sin. For my iniquities have gone over my head; like a heavy burden, they are too heavy for me. My wounds stink and fester because of my foolishness, I am utterly bowed down and prostrate; all the day I go about mourning. For my sides are filled with burning, and there is no soundness in my flesh. I am feeble and crushed; I groan because of the tumult of my heart. O Lord, all my longing is before you; my sighing is not hidden from you. My heart throbs; my strength fails me, and the light of my eyes--it also has gone from me. My friends and companions stand aloof from my plague, and my nearest kin stand far off. Those who seek my life lay their snares; those who seek my hurt speak of ruin and meditate treachery all day long. But I am like a deaf man; I do not hear, like a mute man who does not open his mouth. I have become like a man who does not hear, and in whose mouth are no rebukes.

Psalms 38:1-14

REFLECTIONS

DAY 23

ACCEPTING CHANGE

PSALM 38:15-22

Our society thrives on change and progress. Each year our lives become more advanced, our knowledge grows and our behaviors change. Think about how things have changed in your lifetime, let alone how they've changed since your parents or grandparents were kids. Yet, despite how society embraces and recognizes the positive benefits of change many people believe after a certain point people won't change.

Has your crime or sin become your defining attribute? "Don't trust him, he embezzled." "That guy's an addict, I don't want anything to do with him." "She's a slut, you never know what she might do next."

Before our repentance their comments were right. We shouldn't deny the truth of our past **BUT** that's not our present reality. Like David, we are surrounded by the pain of sin, ready to fall into the abyss of Hell if it wasn't for God's love!

As we confess our sins God hears us, forgives us and changes us! Instead of rejecting change and forsaking us God changes us, stays with us, helps us and saves us!

Now in Him through our changed lives we follow after God!

PRAYER

Almighty God,

My past sins can haunt me. Satan can make me think that I haven't changed enough or You can't make me good enough. Strengthen me to accept the change You have created in my life so I may boldly live in Your goodness.

In Jesus Name I Pray,

Amen

But for you, O LORD, do I wait; it is you, O Lord my God, who will answer. For I said, "Only let them not rejoice over me, who boast against me when my foot slips!" For I am ready to fall, and my pain is ever before me. I confess my iniquity; I am sorry for my sin. But my foes are vigorous, they are mighty, and many are those who hate me wrongfully. Those who render me evil for good accuse me because I follow after good. Do not forsake me, O LORD! O my God, be not far from me! Make haste to help me, O Lord, my salvation!

Psalms 38:15-22

REFLECTIONS

DAY 24

BLESSED CONFESSION

PSALM 32:1-5

When the detectives questioned me about my crimes I had a choice to confess or deny. After my initial fear and denials I confessed. I didn't deny any evidence they showed me. It was freeing and hard. My lawyer had to encourage me constantly not to fight it. I had to own my sins in a very public way because of all the media attention. But, in the process of confessing my guilt and sins the shackles of power that Satan had trapped me with were broken by god's forgiveness!

The words of David ring all too true for us. When we keep silent about our sin and don't confess it to God it will destroy us (v3-4). When we finally reach the point of telling God about our sin instead of receiving the condemnation we expect we are liberated from Satan's power by God's forgiveness. (v5) Not only have we been forgiven but now we have been transformed from "sinner against God" to "blessed child of God"! Our sins are covered (v1) not by the goodness of our confession but by the blood of Christ's sacrifice for us. Thank God for the blessed offering of Christ!

PRAYER

Gracious God,

Thank You for loving me so much that any sin I confess You will cover with forgiveness through the blood of Christ. Send Your Holy Spirit to strengthen me so I may confess my sins to You and receive Your blessing of forgiveness.

In Jesus Name I Pray,

Amen

Blessed is the one whose transgression is forgiven, whose sin is covered. Blessed is the man against whom the LORD counts no iniquity, and in whose spirit there is no deceit. For when I kept silent, my bones wasted away through my groaning all day long. For day and night your hand was heavy upon me; my strength was dried up as by the heat of summer. Selah. I acknowledged my sin to you, and I did not cover my iniquity; I said, "I will confess my transgressions to the LORD," and you forgave the iniquity of my sin.

Psalms 32:1-5

REFLECTIONS

DAY 25

NO SALVATION

PSALM 3:1-4

"You're gonna burn in **HELL!**"

After our sins became public many of us may have heard those words from people we knew or just random folks in our community. Words of condemnation are hard to hear. When others proclaim you've done so much bad that God has no choice but to send you to hell, well, to put it mildly, it can be depressing. If there's no hope in God, in what can I hope?

They make sense, though. Why should we still hope in God? Our sins are great-sins we chose to commit. We're not innocent. Maybe, like David hears from his enemies, there is no salvation for us?

But God hasn't deserted us! Even in our sin God is there like a shield to protect us from the eternal punishment of Hell. God hears our calls of despair when the world tells us we have no hope of salvation. He sends His Holy Spirit to lift our heads out of depression and into His hope filled presence.

Now, when you hear others condemning you remember that they don't have that power. Even more, your God has claimed you as His own through Christ's blood!

PRAYER

Gracious Lord,

Condemning words from the world bring me down and cause me to question my salvation. Send Your Holy Spirit to comfort me by reminding me that You alone have the power to condemn and redeem and You have chosen to redeem me by the blood of Christ.

In Jesus Name I Pray,

Amen

A Psalm of David, when he fled from Absalom his son. O LORD, how many are my foes! Many are rising against me; many are saying of my soul, there is no salvation for him in God. Selah. But you, O LORD, are a shield about me, my glory, and the lifter of my head. I cried aloud to the LORD, and he answered me from his holy hill.

Psalms 3:1-4

REFLECTIONS

DAY 26

LOVING MERCY

PSALM 51:1-2

The prophet Nathan confronts King David with the king's sin of adultery and murder. Since David is the king he doesn't answer to anyone but God for his crimes. In today's Psalm David pleads for mercy from our almighty God. Most all of us pled for mercy at one time or another. We might have begged a judge for probation or less jail time. Maybe you begged a spouse, parent or landlord not to kick you out after some offense. Maybe you begged a boss or teacher for one more chance. If you were lucky enough to receive mercy from someone it usually would come with conditions. Your official punishment might be reduced but you still had to live with people knowing what you did and them treating you differently.

God doesn't hold grudges against David when He responds to David's pleas for loving mercy. The rest of David's life is filled with family strife because of his sin but his eternal place in God's family is secured by God's steadfast love. Likewise, when you plead to God for loving mercy in the midst of earthly strife God hears your prayer and forgives and restores you!

PRAYER

Oh Merciful God,

I have sinned against You. I beg You to show me Your steadfast love and forgive me of my sins so that You purify me and bring me into Your eternal, loving presence.

In Jesus Name I Pray,

Amen

To the choirmaster. A Psalm of David, when Nathan the prophet went to him, after he had gone in to Bathsheba. Have mercy on me, O God, according to your steadfast love; according to your abundant mercy blot out my transgressions. Wash me thoroughly from my iniquity, and cleanse me from my sin!

Psalms 51:1-2

REFLECTIONS

DAY 27

FROM SIN TO WISDOM

PSALM 51:3-6

What do you know? You might think you don't know that much, especially compared to the huge amount of stuff in the universe. But, I bet you know more than you think. You know how to eat. You know how to listen. You know you exist. You know the color of the sky. I could go on but I'll name just one more: you know how to sin.

Knowing how to sin isn't something we like to think about but it's as instinctive as breathing. We don't even think about it. Because of the "original sin" of Adam and Eve, sin is part of who we are. It's constantly separating us from God. We know sin all too well.

God calls us to know something more powerful than sin: His wisdom. It's not a human wisdom based on figuring out stuff by what we see. God's wisdom is the knowledge of His love for us shown in Christ's death and resurrection for our sins. This remains a secret wisdom to many because they refuse to accept that they're sinners or that Jesus died for them. But, for those who believe, it is God's blessed wisdom that brings eternal life and delight!

PRAYER

Dear All Knowing Father,

This world is full of sin and at times I feel this is all I know. Bring me from knowing only sin to knowing Your wisdom revealed in Christ on the cross so I may know You love me and have saved me.

In Jesus Name I Pray,

Amen

For I know my transgressions, and my sin is ever before me. Against you, you only, have I sinned and done what is evil in your sight, so that you may be justified in your words and blameless in your judgment. Behold, I was brought forth in iniquity, and in sin did my mother conceive me. Behold, you delight in truth in the inward being, and you teach me wisdom in the secret heart.

Psalms 51:3-6

REFLECTIONS

DAY 28

STAYING ON GOD'S GOOD SIDE

PSALM 51:7-12

You stay on someone's "good side" by being nice to them, doing what they ask and respecting them. When you don't do these you end up on their bad side and become the object of their anger! If you get on the bad side of your landlord you end up homeless. If you get on the bad side of the law you get locked up. If you get on the bad side of the c.o. or deputy you end up in the hole. What if you get on God's bad side? All these other situation are temporary but getting on God's bad side lands you in Hell.

How do we stay on God's good side?

We can't. At least not on our own.

As sinners from birth we should have been on God's bad side from day one-but that's not where God wants you! God does incredible things for you to stay on His good side. God makes (and keeps) you clean by Christ's blood. He gives you a clean heart, renewed spirit and the Holy Spirit. God fills you with the joy of salvation. God does all this for you to keep you on His good side so He can spend eternity with you!

PRAYER

Almighty God,

I do so many things to get on Your bad side but in Your mercy You constantly forgive me, renew me and restore me so I can stay on Your good side. Send me Your Holy Spirit so I may live strong in Your new life and stay on Your good side for eternity.

In Jesus Name I Pray,

Amen

Purge me with hyssop, and I shall be clean; wash me, and I shall be whiter than snow. Let me hear joy and gladness; let the bones that you have broken rejoice. Hide your face from my sins, and blot out all my iniquities. Create in me a clean heart, O God, and renew a right spirit within me. Cast me not away from your presence, and take not your Holy Spirit from me. Restore to me the joy of your salvation, and uphold me with a willing spirit.

Psalms 51:7-12

REFLECTIONS

DAY 29

YOUR STORY

PSALM 51:12-17

Our lives are stories filled with comedy and suspense. At times the action is fast paced then it may seem to drag on forever. No matter how you feel about your story, you can be sure of this: God uses your story to declare His praise.

You may look at your life and think, "after all I've done how do I declare God's praise? Who would listen to me after what I've done?"

True, not everyone will listen to your declarations of praise. Then again, not everyone listened to Jesus so you're in good company! Besides, your sins aren't the end, or even middle, of your story. They're just the beginning. The middle of your story is when God reveals Himself to you-the sinner. When your sinful spirit broke God created a new live for you. When you began to sing God's praises.

Your story of receiving a new life from God-forgiveness through Christ, strength by the Holy Spirit and the presence of the Father's love-is one that needs to be heard precisely because of what you were before God redeemed you! And the end of your story? What s when you enter heaven for an eternity of peace and joy!

PRAYER

Gracious God,

Use my story, the tale of Your love transforming me and giving me new life, to proclaim Your love and teach Your will to other sinners so You might save them through faith and baptism like You've saved me.

In Jesus Name I Pray,

Amen

Restore to me the joy of your salvation, and uphold me with a willing spirit. Then I will teach transgressors your ways, and sinners will return to you. Deliver me from bloodguiltiness, O God, O God of my salvation, and my tongue will sing aloud of your righteousness. O Lord, open my lips, and my mouth will declare your praise. For you will not delight in sacrifice, or I would give it; you will not be pleased with a burnt offering. The sacrifices of God are a broken spirit; a broken and contrite heart, O God, you will not despise.

Psalms 51:12-17

REFLECTIONS

DAY 30

LIGHT IN THE DARKNESS

PSALM 139:11-12

Being locked up can bring us to some dark places, but not the way I expected. My cell never got dark, even at night with dimmer lights it was still as light as a cloudy afternoon. But the physical brightness couldn't hide the personal darkness.

The darkness of being locked up made me feel covered by the night in a forgotten place. The feeling didn't happen suddenly but crept up on me like the progression from afternoon to dusk to night. You don't notice it happening until it's done and you're hidden in the dark. People don't write to you like they did at first, calls are harder to connect, the darkness becomes isolating. When you feel isolated from others then you can feel isolated from God, too. You feel forgotten in the darkness.

Yet even when "darkness shall cover me" (v11) and my days feel dark like night God sees us clearly as on a sunny day. Since God sees through our darkness God can comfort us even when we feel isolated. God's love is brighter than our personal darkness, bright enough to shine through Satan's clouds of deception and doubt and bright enough to guide us into the unending light of His presence.

PRAYER

Dear Loving Father,

My sin covers me in darkness and I feel lost and alone. Send Your light in to my life so that I may praise You because the light of Your Word overcomes any darkness-even Satan's darkness.

In Jesus Name I Pray,

Amen

If I say, "Surely the darkness shall cover me, and the light about me be night," even the darkness is not dark to you; the night is bright as the day, for darkness is as light with you.

Psalms 139:11-12

REFLECTIONS

DAY 31

PRAISING GOD FOR MAKING ME

PSALM 139:13-16

When the reality of sin hits, you feel worthless. Before my arrest I struggled with depression that came from knowing my sinful and illegal acts. I wondered, "How could God have created me?"

After my arrest I confronted all those feelings in public. I couldn't get a good job, friends abandoned me, people rejected me. Have you felt worthless as you've faced your sins?

The devil uses our struggles to pull us away from God. He tells us we're not good enough for God's love, we're mistakes-God would never make someone capable of doing those things or there's no God and my actions prove it.

But there's another, more powerful, voice. God. God tells you that you were made by Him. God tells you He knows all your days-your days of sin, days of repentance and days of righteousness. Living in the days of our sin, God's proclamation of forgiveness and righteousness might sound like a far off, even imaginary, time. But it's already happened!

In Christ's sacrifice God took us from a prison of hopeless sin to the freedom of forgiveness and righteousness. When you hear Satan's voice, praise God for making you because God knows you today, your yesterdays, your tomorrows and forever!

PRAYER

Loving Father,

Despite my sins and doubts You proclaim to me that I was fearfully and wonderfully made by You. When Satan tries to deceive me give me wisdom to see Your creative work in me so I may always praise you!

In Jesus Name I Pray,

Amen

For you formed my inward parts; you knitted me together in my mother's womb. I praise you, for I am fearfully and wonderfully made. Wonderful are your works; my soul knows it very well. My frame was not hidden from you, when I was being made in secret, intricately woven in the depths of the earth. Your eyes saw my unformed substance; in your book were written, every one of them, the days that were formed for me, when as yet there was none of them.

Psalms 139:13-16

REFLECTIONS

DAY 32

WE'VE GOT A TOUGH LIFE

PSALM 102:8-13

The incarceration life is tough. We can't hide behind a façade, or false front, of "goodness." There are probably hundreds, if not thousands, of folks who sin like you but are never revealed. For some reason God let your sins become known. Now you suffer because of it. Does that mean I can blame God for my tough life?

It sounds appealing, doesn't it? God's the one that made me so God's to blame. God's the one who made the laws so God's to blame. Ultimately, God is the who allowed my sins to become public so God's ultimately the one to blame for my tough life. God took me up and threw me down because of His indignation and anger. (v10)

But God's not done with us yet. The sin-caused suffering of this tough life leads to experiencing God's pity and favor! (v13) Jesus didn't die for the perfectly comfortable but for suffering sinners like us. In God's awesome power God moves us from a tough life filled with sin into the joyful presence of His love. Then, this tough life will be a distant memory as we share God's love forever!

PRAYER

Loving Father,

My sin filled life has brought me suffering. But You have promised me restoration through Jesus. Send Your Holy Spirit to comfort me during my suffering so I may then experience Your loving presence.

In Jesus Name I Pray,

Amen

All the day my enemies taunt me; those who deride me use my name for a curse. For I eat ashes like bread and mingle tears with my drink, because of your indignation and anger; for you have taken me up and thrown me down. My days are like an evening shadow; I wither away like grass. But you, O LORD, are enthroned forever; you are remembered throughout all generations. You will arise and have pity on Zion; it is the time to favor her; the appointed time has come.

Psalms 102:8-13

REFLECTIONS

David Smith

DAY 33

ORPHANS, WIDOWS AND PRISONERS

PSALM 68:4-6

Orphans, widows and prisoners. Those aren't three groups society usually puts together. We see widows and orphans as having a bad lot in life, faultlessly in need of mercy and love. While prisoners, like you and I, get what we deserve. Yet in this Psalm David groups together orphans, widows and prisoners. The world is more likely to group "prisoners" with "rebellious" but David ensures we see these two as separate groups. How can this be?

One becomes a prisoner not because he's rebellious but because either Satan deceived him into sinning or he's suffering under unrighteous rulers. When we see the prisoner this way we have compassion for ourselves and others instead of contempt. Just like a simple piece of bad luck can make you a widow or orphan, a simple deception by Satan can make you a prisoner. Just like God cares for widows and orphans, God cares for prisoners because we need God's love and care.

Now look at this promise to the prisoner-to lead him to prosperity. (v6) This goes against society's promise to the prisoner! It shows us God's love for prisoners and models how we can love other prisoners.

PRAYER

Gracious Lord,

I may despise myself or others who are in prison but you do not. You promise to lead us from bondage to prosperity. Grant me patience and hope to see Your promise fulfilled in my life.

In Jesus Name I Pray,

Amen

Sing to God, sing praises to his name; lift up a song to him who rides through the deserts; his name is the LORD; exult before him! Father of the fatherless and protector of widows is God in his holy habitation. God settles the solitary in a home; he leads out the prisoners to prosperity, but the rebellious dwell in a parched land.

Psalms 68:4-6

REFLECTIONS

DAY 34

GOD'S MERCY FOR GOD'S SAKE

PSALM 6:4-7

Why should someone show you mercy? At a sentencing hearing you see a parade of people appear before the judge telling stories of how the condemned person did a lot of good things in his life and has the ability and desire to do more good things and no longer do the bad things he was convicted of doing. Basically, the guilty guy is asking the judge to have mercy on him for his own sake. Sometimes it works, sometimes it doesn't. But does that same approach work with God? Will God have mercy on you (forgive your sins) if you tell God all the good stuff you've done and promise not to sin again?

No!

Once we sin, which we all did before we can remember, we've separated ourselves from God and there's nothing we can do to convince God to have mercy on us for our own sake.

But God will have mercy on us for His sake!

The Lord hears our prayers and pleas and saves us for the sake of His steadfast love! (v4) God wants to be in your presence and hear your praises forever! God loves you and will show you mercy for His sake!

PRAYER

Almighty God,

Though I try there is nothing I can do to earn Your mercy; therefore I call on You to remember Your steadfast love for me, forgive me because of Christ's death and resurrection and equip me with the Holy Spirit to live a life that praises You!

In Jesus Name I Pray,

Amen

Turn, O LORD, deliver my life; save me for the sake of your steadfast love. For in death there is no remembrance of you; in Sheol who will give you praise? I am weary with my moaning; every night I flood my bed with tears; I drench my couch with my weeping. My eye wastes away because of grief; it grows weak because of all my foes.

Psalms 6:4-7

REFLECTIONS

DAY 35

SINGING PRAISES

PSALM 118:14-18

When do you "sing praises"? Maybe when you get married, have kids or celebrate some milestone in life. It's easy to sing God's praises when things go well but what about now as you suffer because of your sins?

It's not easy when you've been separated from what you love, lost your job or reputation and are locked up. These aren't joyful times but times of suffering. We think, "How can I praise God now?" What if we see this not as a time of suffering but as a time of Godly correction?

God hasn't abandoned you to suffer because of your sins. God's using this time to transform you. Through Christ's blood God has forgiven you. Through God's gifts of belief and baptism God gives you new life. Now through the blessing of God's discipline God is ridding you of Satan's influence and sin.

You may feel on the verge of death but you're living a new life!

Now is the time to sing songs and praise God. God has taken you from a place of sin to His glorious presence-from death to life! Let's sing about this-even in our cells and dorms!

PRAYER

Oh, Almighty God,

The suffering I'm now living with seems unbearable, like You have abandoned me. Yet I know You have saved me and this is really a time of discipline. Thank you for caring so much for me that You make me a better person and let me sing Your praises during days of suffering and of blessing.

In Jesus Name I Pray,

Amen

The LORD is my strength and my song; he has become my salvation. Glad songs of salvation are in the tents of the righteous: "The right hand of the LORD does valiantly, the right hand of the LORD exalts, the right hand of the LORD does valiantly!" I shall not die, but I shall live, and recount the deeds of the LORD. The LORD has disciplined me severely, but he has not given me over to death.

Psalms 118:14-18

REFLECTIONS

DAY 36

WHAT'S NEXT?

PSALM 118:17-24

Eventually we get to a point where we realize our reality. We finally see our sin. We see the punishment and consequences for our sins. We see that God is very present in our lives, although not in a way we enjoy. Then we ask ourselves, "What's next?"

"What's next?" is a question we need to ask because when we repent and believe in Christ's sacrifice for us it means that our current state of being disciplined by God won't last forever. We won't die an eternal death. No, even with our past sins we live forever because of God's love!(v17)

This life is different than what we used to live. Instead of being led by Satan's lies our good shepherd now leads us in His love. God opens the gates of righteousness that lead us to the Lord's presence. (v19) On our own we could never do this but God has done it because God loves us!

God loves us sinners. How amazing is that?

Our God wants our praise right now, even after everything we've done against Him. This is the day the Lord has made, let us rejoice and be glad in it! (v24)

PRAYER

Most Merciful Lord,

Help me to see that Your discipline doesn't last forever. One day You will open the gates of righteousness to me for Christ's sake and I will be in Your pure and holy presence. Until that day, help me say, "This is the day the Lord has made, let us rejoice and be glad in it!"

In Jesus Name I Pray,

Amen

I shall not die, but I shall live, and recount the deeds of the LORD. The LORD has disciplined me severely, but he has not given me over to death. Open to me the gates of righteousness, that I may enter through them and give thanks to the LORD. This is the gate of the LORD; the righteous shall enter through it. I thank you that you have answered me and have become my salvation. The stone that the builders rejected has become the cornerstone. This is the LORD's doing; it is marvelous in our eyes. This is the day that the LORD has made; let us rejoice and be glad in it.

Psalms 118:17-24

REFLECTIONS

DAY 37

REJOICING TO SALVATION

PSALM 118:24-25

"Don't count your chickens before they hatch," "take it one day at a time," "don't get ahead of yourself!" How many times has someone told you something like one of these? These sayings can be helpful if we get too prideful or are lusting after the future. But when we're living in the midst of God's discipline we **need** to look to the future. We need to get "ahead of ourselves" so we can know that God is lovingly correcting us and not wrathfully tormenting us.

In the midst of his troubles the psalmist cries out to God, "save us"! (v25) He also says, "This is the day the Lord has made, let us rejoice and be glad in it." (v24) The psalmist knows his future salvation so he can praise God now. We know our future salvation because it's a present reality through Christ. We can praise God right now, too! It doesn't matter that we've been separated from our loved ones, rejected by society or may even have no hope to live outside prison walls-we have a savior who loves us, saved us and will give us a holy success beyond our wildest dreams!

PRAYER

All-knowing and All-powerful God,

Do not let me be burdened by my present suffering but let me rejoice now, during my disciplining by revealing to me the reality of my salvation in Christ so I may rejoice and be glad in the day You've given me!

In Jesus Name I Pray,

Amen

This is the day that the LORD has made; let us rejoice and be glad in it. Save us, we pray, O LORD! O LORD, we pray, give us success!
Psalms 118:24-25

REFLECTIONS

DAY 38

FAST COMPASSION

PSALM 79:8-9

It sometimes seems that the only times that happen quickly are the ones that cause pain. Others knowing about your sins, the legal punishment for what you've done or even the thought that God no longer cares for you because of what you've done can happen sooner than you want.

The bad things come so quickly they can distract you from the good. Satan uses these consequences to trick you into doubting God's love for you or the compassion God feels towards you. Despite Satan's lies God, your loving Father, promises a fast compassion!

It's a fast compassion because neither you nor Satan can slow it down or get in its way. It's all of God's love and mercy coming directly to you in the midst of your sin, no matter how far Satan has pulled you down!

God's fast compassion for you glorifies God. It shows God's power over Satan and creation. For His name's sake God makes us right with Him because God doesn't want to wait for your love: not for a year, a month or even a week. Right now God's fast compassion is coming for you-even behind these walls!

PRAYER

Almighty God,

In the midst of my sin I beg you to come quickly and pull me up from the depths that Satan has drug me to. Show me your compassion quickly so I may be restored and praise You always!

In Jesus Name I Pray,

Amen

Do not remember against us our former iniquities; let your compassion come speedily to meet us, for we are brought very low. Help us, O God of our salvation, for the glory of your name; deliver us, and atone for our sins, for your name's sake!

Psalms 79:8-9

REFLECTIONS

DAY 39

BOLD CALL FOR GRACE

PSALM 6:1-3

Grace and mercy are two words we use a lot to describe how God deals with us sinners. Both have to do with God's loving actions towards us. "Mercy" is God withholding the punishment we deserve while "grace" is God giving you an undeserved gift. Mercy is about what we don't get and grace is about what we do get.

The grace that God gives us makes today's Psalm incredible! Here is David suffering under the punishment of his sin. He knows God is disciplining him. David could simply ask for mercy, for God to withhold the punishing discipline. Instead, David boldly asks for grace. He doesn't just call on God to withhold punishment but also to bless him with grace!

That means as we're suffering through God's discipline we can still boldly call out for grace! Just as a parent doesn't stop loving a child during "time out," God doesn't stop loving us while we suffer through the adult version of timeout: incarceration.

Like David we may have to wait to experience God's grace (v3) but through Christ we have God's promise of abundant grace!

PRAYER

Gracious God,

In my self-induced sin fed suffering I call out to You not just for mercy to deliver me from my suffering but also grace to bless me with Your abundant love through Christ. Keep me strong in Your Spirit now as I await Your grace filled blessings.

In Jesus Name I Pray,

Amen

O LORD, rebuke me not in your anger, nor discipline me in your wrath. Be gracious to me, O LORD, for I am languishing; heal me, O LORD, for my bones are troubled. My soul also is greatly troubled. But you, O LORD--how long?

Psalms 6:1-3

REFLECTIONS

DAY 40

FROM BAD TO BETTER

PSALM 60:1-4

From bad to worse-isn't that how life seems to go? You lose your job then you can't pay rent. You get arrested for one crime then something worse is alleged. You go through the public humiliation of an arrest and expect a lenient judge then end up with a harsh sentence. From bad to worse may be how our lives seem to go but with God we go from bad to better.

In today's Psalm David laments that God has rejected him and Israel because of their sins. Their defenses are broken and army decimated. It seems things are bad and can only get worse. But David knows with God things go from bad to better.

David sees God's promise of safety in troubled times when he says, "you have set up a banner for those who fear you that they may to it." (v4)

Even though God is angry, God still loves us! God has a place of protection for us at the cross. The cross of Christ is our banner that we flee to! Here we find not only safety but love and hope. At the cross God takes us from bad to better!

PRAYER

Almighty God,

In my sin you rejected me and my life seems to be going from bad to worse. But in Your mercy Christ died for me and is Your banner of safety in my troubled times. Draw me to Your banner so I might experience Your love and go from bad to better.

In Jesus Name I Pray,

Amen

A Miktam of David; for instruction; when he strove with Aram-naharaim and with Aram-zobah, and when Joab on his return struck down twelve thousand of Edom in the Valley of Salt.

O God, you have rejected us, broken our defenses; you have been angry; oh, restore us. You have made the land to quake; you have torn it open; repair its breaches, for it totters. You have made your people see hard things; you have given us wine to drink that made us stagger. You have set up a banner for those who fear you, that they may flee to it from the bow. Selah.

Psalms 60:1-4

REFLECTIONS

David Smith

SCRIPTURE INDEX

MORE RESOURCES FOR INCARCERATED INDIVIDUALS AND THEIR LOVED ONES

If you would like to discover more devotionals and other resources for incarcerated individuals and their loved ones visit www.inthrive.us

ABOUT THE AUTHOR

David Smith was a pastor for 6 years until the day he was arrested. He subsequently spent 2 ½ years incarcerated, including over 16 months in solitary. During that time God transformed his life and David experienced God's Word in a powerful and life giving way. He now works to provide support and hope to individuals affected by incarceration and their loved ones.

Made in the USA
Coppell, TX
15 March 2025

47152636R00056